Traditional Black Music

SPIRITUALS

CHELSEA HOUSE PUBLISHERS
New York   Philadelphia

On the cover Spirituals are songs of lasting power and continuing relevance. As a result, they have been passed down from one generation of African Americans to the next.

Chelsea House Publishers

EDITORIAL DIRECTOR   Richard Rennert

EXECUTIVE MANAGING EDITOR   Karyn Gullen Browne

COPY CHIEF   Robin James

PICTURE EDITOR   Adrian G. Allen

CREATIVE DIRECTOR   Robert Mitchell

ART DIRECTOR   Joan Ferrigno

PRODUCTION MANAGER   Sallye Scott

Staff for Spirituals

ASSISTANT EDITOR   Mary Sisson

EDITORIAL ASSISTANT   Scott D. Briggs

PICTURE RESEARCHER   Villette Harris

BOOK LAYOUT   Lydia Rivera

First Printing

1   3   5   7   9   8   6   4   2

Library of Congress Cataloging-in-Publication Data

Spirituals / [compiled by] Jerry Silverman.
1 score. — (Traditional Black music)
For voice and piano: includes chord symbols.
Includes index.
ISBN 0-7910-1838-5   0-7910-1854-7 (pbk)
1. Spirituals (Songs)—Juvenile. [1. Spirituals (Songs) music. 2. Afro-Americans—Music.] I. Silverman, Jerry. II. Series.
M1670.S755 1995   # 32487914   94-43649
                                                       CIP
                                                       ACM

PICTURE CREDITS
The Bettmann Archive: pp. 5, 9, 13, 19, 29, 41, 55, 59;
UPI/Bettmann: pp. 23, 37, 47.

CONTENTS

Author's Preface

The body of songs known as the Negro Spiritual contain the most profound sentiments of the people who created and sang them—the enslaved Africans of the American South. These songs combine the feelings of suffering and despair caused by the brutal and inhumane slave system with the hope, defiance, and even joy of an indomitable people who refused to lose faith in the promise of a better life and ultimate redemption.

If spirituals consisted only of words, they would make for some fascinating reading in a course in social history or theology. But spirituals also contain some of the most sublime melodies to spring from the human genius—melodies that weep and cry, that laugh and exult. They are marvels of tonal invention. They contain broad, sweeping phrases and syncopated jagged edges. They cause bodies to sway, feet to stamp, hands to clap, and voices to be raised on high.

Heroes from the Old Testament abound in spirituals, giving advice and setting examples. When Moses was told by God to lead the children of Israel out of bondage, African Americans took heart. When Joshua's trumpets caused the walls of Jericho to crumble, it seemed clear that slavery's walls would crumble too. When little David won an unequal struggle against a mighty foe, slaves looked at their own struggle with newfound hope.

Sometimes rebellious sentiments led to militant actions, and spirituals became an invaluable means of clandestine communication. If an escape on the Underground Railroad was in the offing, "Steal Away to Jesus" got the message across to those in the know without tipping off hostile parties.

Although they date from the early to mid-19th century, spirituals have survived to our own day because of their relevance to today's struggles. Marian Anderson sang them on the steps of the Lincoln Memorial in Washington, D.C., after having been denied access to a concert hall because of her color. Activists in the civil rights movement of the 1960s picked up spirituals, changed a word here and there, and sang them on freedom rides and sit-ins. Martin Luther King, Jr., quoted their lyrics in his inspiring speeches.

This collection can only scratch the surface of this priceless musical heritage. Yet there is enough material here to give a clear idea of the variety and depth of both the lyrical and musical sentiments that fill each spiritual. It is up to the present-day reader and singer to make these songs come alive once more and to pass them on to future generations.

Jerry Silverman

The Contribution of Blacks to American Art and Culture

Kenneth B. Clark

Historical and contemporary social inequalities have obscured the major contribution of American blacks to American culture. The historical reality of slavery and the combined racial isolation, segregation, and sustained educational inferiority have had deleterious effects. As related pervasive social problems determine and influence the art that any group can not only experience but also, ironically, the extent to which they can eventually contribute to the society as a whole, this tenet is even more visible when assessing the contributions made by African Americans.

All aspects of the arts have been pursued by black Americans, but music provides a special insight into the persistent and inescapable social forces to which black Americans have been subjected. One can speculate that in their preslavery patterns of life in Africa, blacks used rhythm, melody, and lyrics to hold on to reality, hope, and the acceptance of life. Later, in America, music helped blacks endure the cruelties of slavery. Spirituals and gospel music provided a medium for both communion and communication. As the black experience in America became more complex, so too did black music, which has grown and ramified, dramatically affecting the development of American music in general. The result is that today, more than ever before, black music provides a powerful lens through which we may view the history of black Americans in a new and revealing way.

The emotional and religious power of spirituals —both in their touching lyrics and in their forceful melodies—have made them a staple of church services for over a century.

Jordan's River is deep and wide,
Meet my mother on the other side.

The actual Jordan River is neither deep nor wide, but the slaves who sang about crossing over "into campground" were not concerned with topographical details. The "promised land" in this song had a very down-to-earth meaning, that of a land free of slavery. This subversive message had to be hidden behind the biblical geography. But the secular meaning of this song in no way lessens its religious power nor the power of its vision of complete freedom found "at Jesus' feet."

DEEP RIVER

gos - pel feast, That prom - ised land where

all _____ is peace? _____

D.C.

I'll go up to Heaven and take my seat,
And cast my crown at Jesus' feet.   *Chorus*

When I go up to Heaven I'll walk about,
There's nobody there to turn me out.   *Chorus*

Motherless children have a hard time,
When mother is dead.
They ain't got no place to go,
Wander 'round from do' to do' ...

In a sense, all the slaves were "motherless children." They were taken from Mother
Africa and transported "a long way from home," and their families were often broken
up and dispersed. The sense of being a stranger in a strange land must have been
overwhelming. There was also an enormous difference between the ideal world of
the believers and the real world of injustice and hardship in which they lived. As a
result, the "true believer" who is "almost gone" to "that heavenly land" is the one who
feels the most distanced from ordinary life.

SOMETIMES I FEEL LIKE A MOTHERLESS CHILD

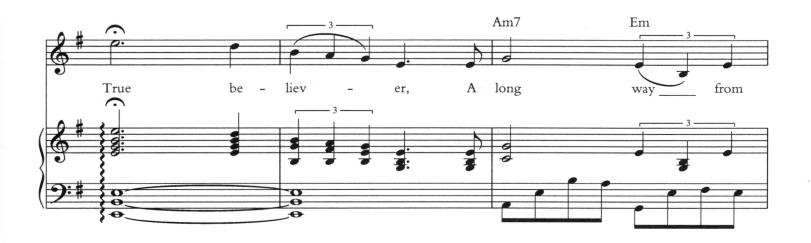

True   be - liev - er,   A   long   way ____ from

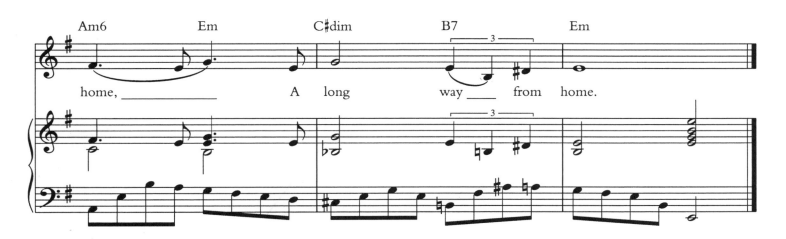

home, _____   A   long   way ____ from   home.

Sometimes I feel like I'm almost gone.
Sometimes I feel like I'm almost gone.
Sometimes I feel like I'm almost gone,
Way up in that heavenly land,
Way up in that heavenly land.
True believer!
Way up in that heavenly land.
Way up in that heavenly land.

Similarly

Sometimes I feel like a feather in the air . . .
A long way from home . . .

Children were not spared
the backbreaking labor
of picking cotton. Even
three- and four-year-olds
were expected to help out
by carrying water to
older workers.

This syncopated, hand-clapping spiritual announces the good news of God's promise with an energy that foreshadows the intensity of gospel music. Peter rings those bells, joy bursts forth, and the singer exclaims, "I heard from heaven today!" But unlike the racing trains and chariots that speed the believer home to God in gospel music, the fulfillment of God's word in this song occurs only after death.

OH, PETER, GO RING THEM BELLS

Oh, Pe - ter, go ring them bells, Pe - ter, go _ ring them bells,

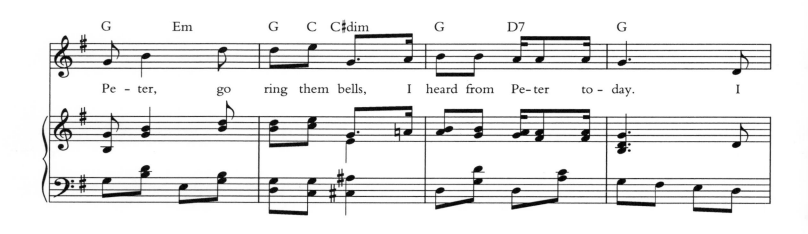

Pe - ter, go ring them bells, I heard from Pe - ter to - day. I

won-der where { my moth - er } is gone. I won-der where { my _ moth - er is gone, I
{ broth - er mos - es } { broth - er Dan - i - el's gone, They're

won-der where my moth-er is gone,
gone _ where E - li - jah is gone,
I heard from Heav- en to - day. I

Chorus

heard from Heav- en to - day, I heard from Heav- en to - day, I

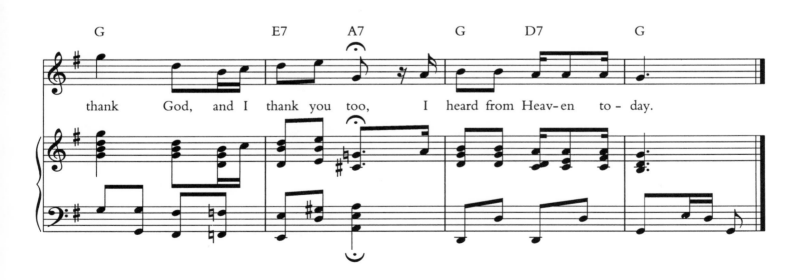

thank God, and I thank you too, I heard from Heav- en to - day.

Way down yonder in the meadow
Lies a poor little lambie;
The bees and the butterflies pickin' out its eyes,
The poor little thing cries, "Mammy."

Spirituals about crying lambs were actually a form of protest song. The children of slaves were often neglected by their mothers, who had to spend their time caring for the children of their masters. Slaves objected in song to this situation, but the protest message had to be hidden. The "lambs all a-cryin" also represented the entire slave population, oppressed but hopeful of a future reward.

LISTEN TO THE LAMBS

ups and downs, _ | Want to go to Heav-en when I die; | An - gels wait -ing for to
be a - shame, _ | | An - gels wait -ing for to
walk the cross, _ | | Foot might slip _ and your

give you a crown, _____ | Want to go to Heav-en when I die. Oh, lis-ten to the
write down your name, _____ |
soul get __ lost. _____ |

D.S. al Fine

A family works the fields in this 1890 photograph. Unfortunately, the abolition of slavery did little to improve the lot of most blacks, and many became impoverished sharecroppers or migrant farm workers.

Good news—chariot's a-comin',
And I don't want it to leave me behind.

The chariot of "Swing Low, Sweet Chariot" recalls the biblical story of the prophet Elijah, who avoided death by being taken up to heaven in a chariot of fire. In order for people to get on board this heaven-bound (or freedom-bound) chariot, it had to come down, or "swing low," to earth. But once it did, only the righteous and holy could get on. The chariot would have no room for sinners.

SWING LOW, SWEET CHARIOT

15

Although some spirituals contained hidden political messages, most of the songs were more concerned with religious life. This song expresses its simple message in a short, thrice-repeated line in the chorus, "I'm a-travling to the grave." The verses tell the story of various loved ones who have gone to glory. There is no secret agenda here, only sorrow tempered by faith in redemption.

I'M A-TRAVLING TO THE GRAVE

shout-ing, ___ sing-ing glo-ry hal - le - lu - jah, ___ The

last words he said to me, was a-bout Je - ru - sa - lem. I'm a -
(she)

D.S. al Fine

Moses, who led the children of Israel out of bondage and to the promised land, was a powerful symbol to the slaves. But this song may very well have been inspired by a latter-day Moses, ex-slave Harriet Tubman. A tireless "conductor" on the Underground Railroad (a group of secret escape routes to the free North), she made scores of journeys into slavery's "Egypt land," returning North each time with a group of runaways. Despite a $40,000 bounty on her head, Tubman was never caught and never lost a "passenger." "Go Down, Moses" was printed in its entirety in the *New York Tribune* in 1861, making it the first spiritual published in the United States.

GO DOWN, MOSES

When Is-rael was in E-gypt's Land, Let my peo-ple go, Op-

pressed so hard they could not stand, Let my peo-ple go.

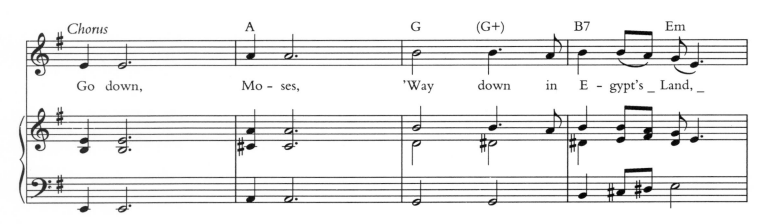

Chorus

Go down, Mo-ses, 'Way down in E-gypt's _ Land, _

Tell ol' Phar - aoh, To let my peo - ple go.

Thus saith the Lord, bold Moses said,
Let my people go,
If not, I'll smite your first-born dead,
Let my people go.   *Chorus*

No more shall they in bondage toil,
Let them come out with Egypt's spoil.   *Chorus*

The Lord told Moses what to do,
To lead the Hebrew children through.   *Chorus*

O come along Moses, you'll not get lost,
Stretch out your rod and come across.   *Chorus*

As Israel stood by the waterside,
At God's command it did divide.   *Chorus*

When they reached the other shore,
They sang a song of triumph o'er.   *Chorus*

Pharaoh said he'd go across,
But Pharaoh and his host were lost.   *Chorus*

Jordan shall stand up like a wall,
And the walls of Jericho shall fall.   *Chorus*

Your foes shall not before you stand,
And you'll possess fair Canaan's Land.   *Chorus*

O let us all from bondage flee,
And let us all in Christ be free.   *Chorus*

We need not always weep and mourn,
And wear these slavery chains forlorn.   *Chorus*

Harriet Tubman (far left) poses with a few of the former slaves she helped escape from the South.
Despite her mild exterior, she had a will of iron, reportedly motivating timid escapees with a pistol.

This song contains an excellent example of the "zipper" format common in many spirituals. The song is set up so that the singer can include ("zip in") as many names in as many verses as the mood dictates. This type of song makes group participation easy. Only one or two words in each new verse is changed, so new verses are easy to sing along with and can be invented instantly.

STANDIN' IN THE NEED OF PRAYER

sis – ter, ___   it's a me, O Lord, _   stand- in' in the need of
moth- er, ___

prayer, _____   stand- in' in the need of   prayer. _____ It's a

D.S. al Fine

In the antebellum South, a seemingly innocuous phrase like "steal away to Jesus" could and did convey information about secret meetings or escape attempts among the slaves. Verses signaled the time and place for the get-together. "Green trees are bending" probably refers to a place for a meeting, while "I ain't got long to stay here" indicates that the time for escape is nigh. This song was reportedly used to arrange meetings by the enslaved men and women who took part in Nat Turner's Rebellion, an uprising in Virginia in 1831.

STEAL AWAY

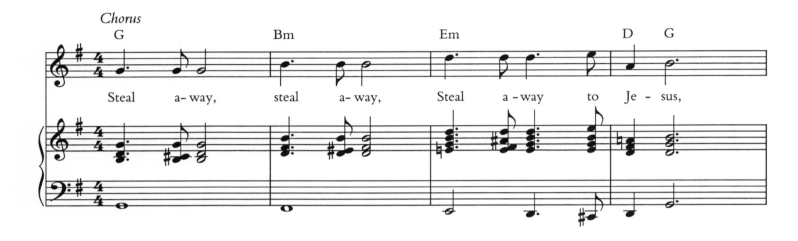

trum-pet sounds with-in-a my soul, I ain't got long to stay here.

Green trees are bending,
Poor sinner stands a-trembling;
The trumpet sounds within-a my soul,
I ain't got long to stay here. *Chorus*

Tombstones are bursting,
Poor sinner stands a-trembling;
The trumpet sounds within-a my soul,
I ain't got long to stay here. *Chorus*

My Lord calls me,
He calls me by the lightning;
The trumpet sounds within-a my soul,
I ain't got long to stay here. *Chorus*

A man and his ox pass through the dirt streets of Richmond, Virginia, the capital of the Confederacy during the Civil War. It was a two-day trip north from Southampton County, where a slave named Nat Turner organized his famous rebellion in 1831.

This song touches on a favorite theme in spirituals and, later, in gospel songs like "No Hiding Place." No matter how hard a sinner tries, God's wrath cannot be avoided. In this song, sinners, fearful of the final judgment, envy the hiding places of the animals and birds. The wise, realizing that they're "bound to leave this world," repent and serve God. The unrepentant look in vain for a place to escape judgment. The song predicts the fate of those who continue in sin: "If you haven't got the grace of God in your heart, the devil will get you sho'."

HARD TRIALS

I'm gonna put on my long white robe,
Down by the riverside.

This rousingly optimistic spiritual nevertheless sounds a note of caution: Not everybody is going to make the long-awaited trip to heaven. But there will be no segregation among those who do succeed. Everyone, rich or poor, black or white, will get a fine robe and crown and will "sing all over God's heav'n."

HEAV'N, HEAV'N

I've got a robe,   you've got a robe,
I've got a crown,   you've got a crown,
I've got a song,   you've got a song,

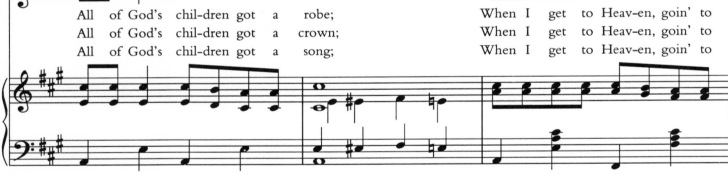

All of God's chil-dren got a   robe;   When I get to Heav-en, goin' to
All of God's chil-dren got a   crown;   When I get to Heav-en, goin' to
All of God's chil-dren got a   song;   When I get to Heav-en, goin' to

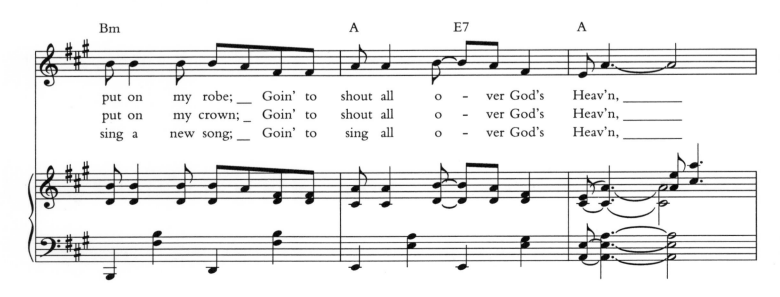

put on   my robe; __ Goin' to   shout all   o - ver God's Heav'n, _____
put on   my crown; _ Goin' to   shout all   o - ver God's Heav'n, _____
sing a   new song; __ Goin' to   sing all   o - ver God's Heav'n, _____

And sixty-three is the jubilee
For the darkies everywhere.

In 1863, during the height of the Civil War, Abraham Lincoln signed the Emancipation Proclamation, abolishing slavery in the South. When the news reached the slaves, they sang of a cloudy way cleared by the angels (the liberating Union army) with "fire in the east and fire in the west." "Go send them angels down" the song demands before proclaiming joyously that "this is the year of the jubilee."

MY WAY'S CLOUDY

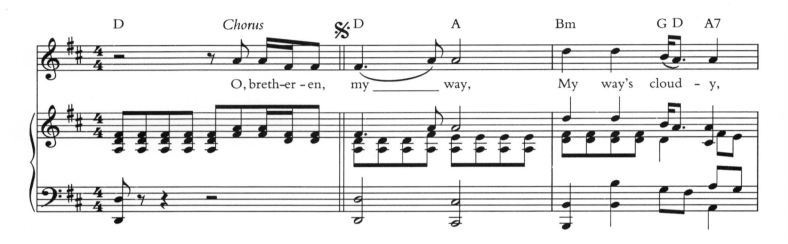

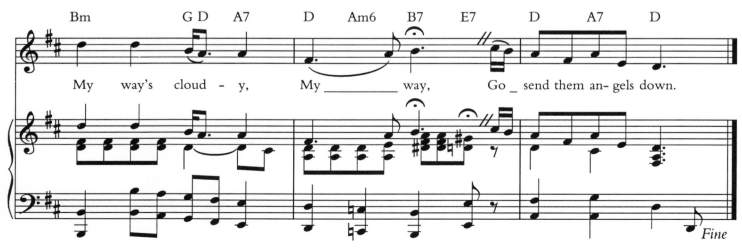

| Verse | Bm | F#m | G | F#m | Bm | E7 | A7 |

There's fire in the east and fire in the west, Send them an - gels down, And
Old Sa - tan is mad and I am so glad, He
This is the year of ju - bi - lee, The

| D | F#7 | Bm | E7 | F#m | E7 | D | A7 |

fire a - mong the Meth - o - dist, O, send them an - gels down. O, breth-er- en,
missed the soul he thought he had, Lord has come to set us free,

D.S. al Fine

Four girls refresh themselves with a drink from a well. Spirituals promised an equally sweet relief from the hard work and drudgery of everyday life.

29

In this song the faithful are invited to "a city into the Heaven." But the slaves who sang it were equally concerned with life here on earth. Songs about pulling down Satan's kingdom and building up the walls of Zion have a nice scriptural ring about them, but they had a contemporary significance as well. Lines like "we will travel on together" or "goin' to war against the devil" took on a different meaning with the rise of the abolitionist movement, the Underground Railroad, and, finally, the Civil War.

I DON'T FEEL NO-WAYS TIRED

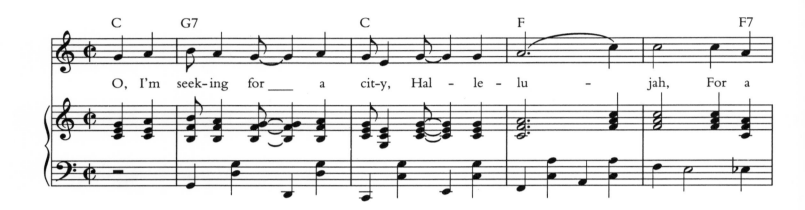

O, I'm seek-ing for ___ a cit-y, Hal - le - lu - jah, For a

cit-y in - to the Heav-en, Hal - le - lu - jah. O,

breth-ren trav - el with me, Hal - le - lu - jah, Say, ___

fire, ___ Chil-dren. O _____ glo - ry Hal - le - lu - jah!

We will travel on together,
    Hallelujah,
Goin' to war agin the devil,
    Hallelujah,
Goin' to pull down Satan's kingdom,
    Hallelujah,
Goin' to build up the walls of Zion,
    Hallelujah.   *Chorus*

The opening lines of this beloved spiritual evoke the pain and suffering of generations of enslaved men, women, and children. They ring out like that earlier supplication, "Lord, why hast Thou forsaken me?" But despite its haunting sadness, this song is not entirely a lament. The opening chorus ends with "Glory Hallelujah!" and the verses describe escaping Satan's power and having sin washed away by Jesus. The message to believers is clear: No matter how hard it gets, God will deliver you from your suffering.

NOBODY KNOWS
THE TROUBLE I'VE SEEN

No-bod - y knows the trou-ble I've seen, No-bo - dy knows but Je - sus.

No-bo - dy knows the trou-ble I've seen, Glo - ry Hal - le - lu jah! Some -

Verse

Fine

times I'm up, some - times I'm down, O, yes, Lord._____ Some -

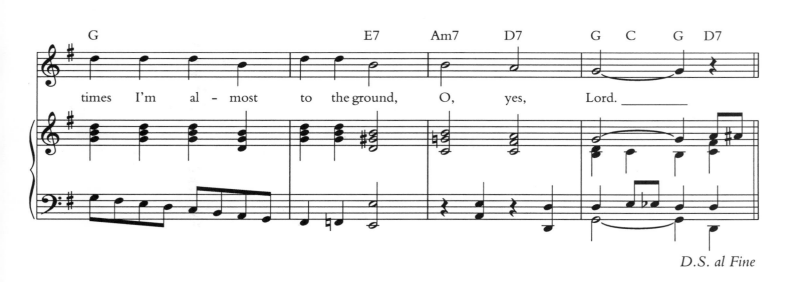

times I'm al - most to the ground, O, yes, Lord._____

D.S. al Fine

Now, you may think that I don't know . . .
But I've had my troubles here below. . . *Chorus*

One day when I was walkin' along . . .
The sky opened up and love came down . . . *Chorus*

What make old Satan hate me so? . . .
He had me once and had to let me go . . . *Chorus*

I never shall forget that day . . .
When Jesus washed my sins away . . . *Chorus*

This rousing spiritual is full of confidence and hope, despite the sorrows and woe of life here on earth. When the Lord spoke to Moses "on the mountain," humanity was shown the righteous way. But people cannot just intellectually understand what is good, they must *feel* the spirit and be moved by its presence. Although people have not always followed the correct path, when feeling believers ask, "Could it be mine?" they are not turned away.

EV'RY TIME I FEEL THE SPIRIT

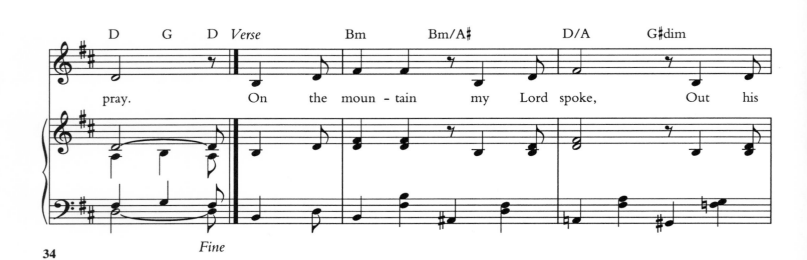

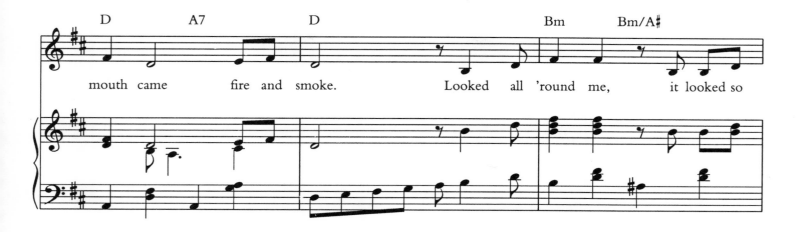

mouth came fire and smoke. Looked all 'round me, it looked so

fine, I asked the Lord, ___ could it be mine. Ev' - ry

D.S. al Fine

Oh, I have sorrows and I have woe,
And I have heart-ache here below;
But while God leads me, I'll never fear,
For I am sheltered by His care. *Chorus*

The word *roll* is a favorite with singers and appears in songs such as "Roll, Jordan, Roll," "When the Roll Is Called Up Yonder," "If You Don't Roll the Devil," and "Roll the Chariot On." Folksinger and raconteur Lee Hays claims that "the word is the best singing sound of all good words that fit well in the voice. It's the beauty of the *o* sound itself; the *r* gives it a good foothold in the throat, and the *ll* tapers it off nice and sweet. A good singer can sing anything, I've heard, but for real topnotch unrefined hightoned singing, give me a song full of *o*'s, preferably surrounded by *r*'s and *l*'s."

I'M A-ROLLING

I'm a - roll - ing, I'm a - roll - ing, I'm a - roll - ing through an un - friend - ly world, ____ I'm a - roll - ing, I'm a - roll - ing through an un - friend - ly world.

Fine

Verse

O broth-ers won't you help me? O broth-ers won't you help me to pray?
O sis-ters won't you help me? O sis-ters won't you help me to pray?
O preach-ers won't you help me? O preach-ers won't you help me to pray?

O broth-ers won't you help me,
O sis-ters won't you help me, } Won't you help me in the ser-vice of the Lord? I'm a
O preach-ers won't you help me,

D.S. al Fine

Legendary contralto Marian Anderson sings before the Lincoln Memorial in Washington, D.C., after being denied the use of a concert hall owned by the Daughters of the American Revolution because of her race. Anderson's Lincoln Memorial concert was a huge success, drawing a record crowd of 75,000 listeners.

A camp meetin' took place
In a wide open space,
Way down in Georgia.

This song exhorts potential converts to "go down in the valley on your knees." This is more than a poetic image; the river valleys were where the newly converted were baptized and where prayer meetings were usually held. The song promises that those who have gathered in the valley "to sing and pray" will have the power to drive away the devil and will be among the few righteous ones to get their crown and get into heaven.

WAIT TILL I PUT ON MY CROWN

Wait 'till I put on my crown, O yes! O yes!

If you want to catch that heavenly breeze,
O yes! O yes!
Go down in the valley on your knees,
O yes! O yes! *Chorus*

Colonel Thomas Wentworth Higginson, who led a regiment of black troops during the Civil War, was an early collector of slave songs. He noted that at the outbreak of the Civil War a group of blacks had been jailed in Georgetown, South Carolina, for singing "My Father, How Long." He wrote: "'We'll soon be free' was too dangerous an assertion, and though the chant was an old one, it was no doubt sung with redoubled emphasis during the new events. 'De Lord will call us home' was evidently thought to be a symbolic verse; for, as a little drummer boy explained it to me, . . . 'Dey tink *de Lord* mean for to say *de Yankees.*'"

MY FATHER, HOW LONG?

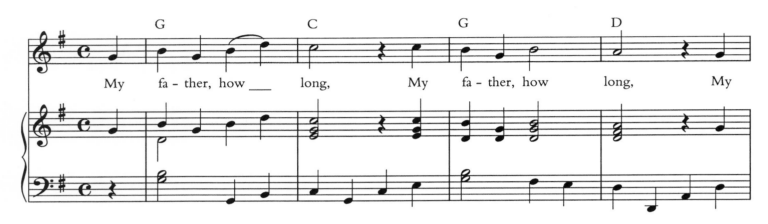

My fa-ther, how ___ long, My fa-ther, how long, My

fa-ther, how long, Poor sin-ner suf - fer here?

Chorus

And it won't be long, And it won't_ be __ long, And it

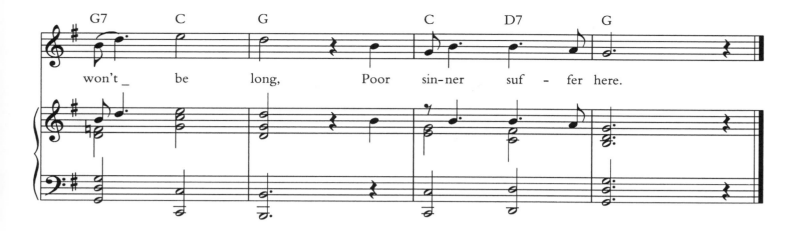

won't _ be long, Poor sin-ner suf – fer here.

We'll soon be free,
We'll soon be free,
We'll soon be free,
The Lord will call us home.   *Chorus*

We'll walk the miry road . . .
Where pleasure never dies.   *Chorus*

We'll walk the golden streets . . .
Of the new Jerusalem.   *Chorus*

My brothers do sing . . .
The praises of the Lord.   *Chorus*

We'll fight for liberty . . .
When the Lord will call us home.   *Chorus*

Songs like "My Father, How Long?" with their sweet melodies and assurances of a better life, helped distract black laborers from repetitive and exhausting work.

On the seventh day,
they rose at the break of dawn
and strode around the city,
in the same manner, seven times.

. . . At the seventh time, the priest sounded the trumpets and Joshua said unto the people: "Raise up your battle cry, for Yahweh has delivered the city unto you!" . . . Then the people raised up their battle cry and they sounded the trumpets. And when the people heard the sound of the trumpet, the people raised up the great battle cry and the wall tumbled down Joshua's victory in the battle of Jericho, as told in Joshua 6: 20–26, is celebrated in this rousing spiritual. The song reassured believers that if they were strong like Joshua, God would help bring the walls of slavery "tumblin' down."

JOSHUA FIT THE BATTLE OF JERICHO

Chorus

Josh - ua fit the bat - tle of _____ Je - ri - cho, __ Je - ri - cho, __

Je - ri - cho, _____ Josh - ua fit the bat - tle of _____ Je - ri - cho __ And the

1. *to Verse*   2. *Final Ending*

walls came tum - bl - in' down. _____ You may down. _____

Fine

42

talk a-bout your king of Gid- e - on, __ talk a-bout your man of Saul, __

__ But there's none like good old Josh - u - a, At the

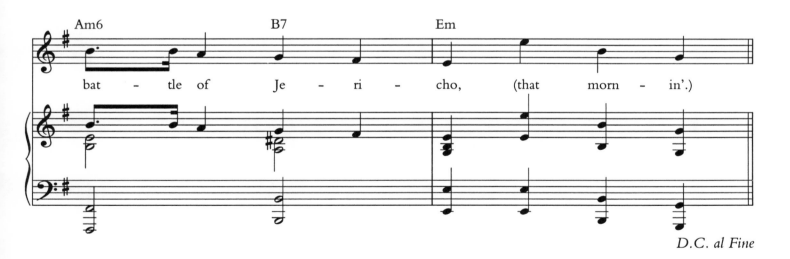

bat - tle of Je - ri - cho, (that morn - in'.)

D.C. al Fine

Up to the walls of Jericho
He marched with spear in hand,
"Go blow those ram-horns," Joshua cried,
"Cause the battle is in my hands."   *Chorus*

Then the lamb, ram, sheephorns began to blow,
The trumpets began to sound.
Joshua commanded the children to shout,
And the walls come a tumbling down.   *Chorus*

There's no man like Joshua
No man like Saul
No man like Joshua
At the battle of Jericho.   *Chorus*

Joining God's army was a common image in spirituals such as "We Are Climbing Jacob's Ladder" and "In the Army of the Lord." The biblical and symbolic language provided a safe way for slaves to express their anger and frustration at their treatment. But this image took on yet another meaning after the passage by Congress of the Militia Act of July 17, 1862. The act authorized the enrollment of "persons of the African descent" in "any military or naval service for which they may be found competent." Now there was a real "gold band" in which African-American men could march and under whose colors they could strike a blow for the freedom of their people.

THE GOLD BAND

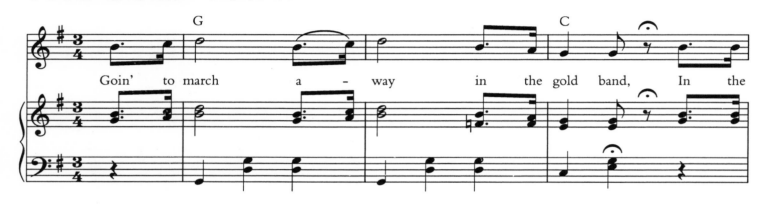

Goin' to march a - way in the gold band, In the

ar - my, bye and bye; Goin' to march a - way in the

gold band, In the ar - my, bye and bye. Sin - ner,

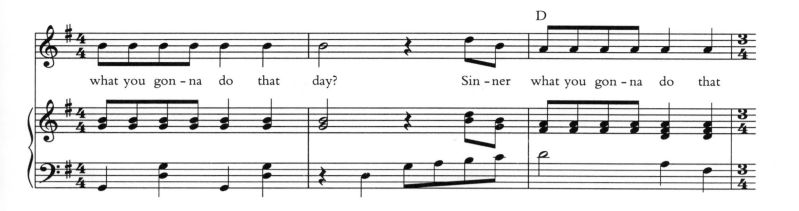

what you gon-na do that day? Sin-ner what you gon-na do that

day? When the fire's a - roll - ing be-

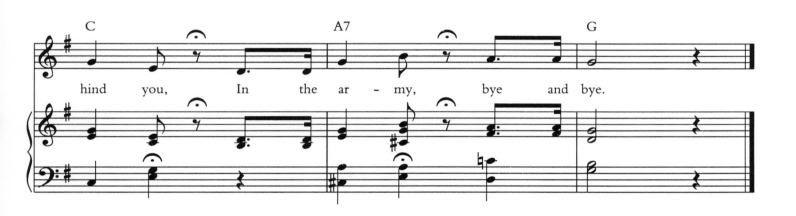

hind you, In the ar - my, bye and bye.

Sister Mary goin' to hand down the robe,
In the army, bye and bye;
Goin' to hand down the robe and the gold band,
In the army, bye and bye. *Chorus*

Jesus was an especially meaningful figure to believing slaves because he too had suffered persecution and torture. He also offered the hope of deliverance from such trials. Consequently, he is a fitting guide on the road to heaven. But Jesus is not merely a guide in this song. He is part of the community of believers that will gather by the water to pray and baptize converts. This community is open to anyone, and outsiders are repeatedly invited to "join in the band."

JESUS ON THE WATER-SIDE

Heav'n bell a-ring, I know de road, Heav'n bell a-ring, I know de road;

Heav'n bell a-ring, I know de road, Je-sus sit-tin' on de wa-ter-side.

Do come a-long, do let us go, Do come a-long, do let us go,
Don't stay be-hind, Don't stay be-hind,
Join in the band, Join in the band,

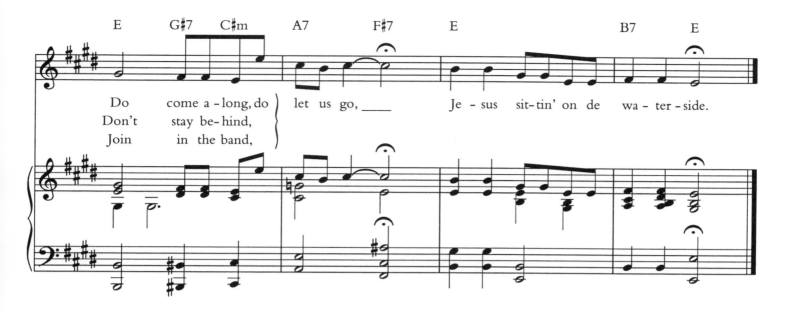

Do come a-long, do let us go, ___ Je-sus sit-tin' on de wa-ter-side.
Don't stay be-hind,
Join in the band,

A woman is baptized in a creek in Virginia. Baptisms and prayer meetings were usually held near such bodies of water; images of the river and the river valley appear in a number of spirituals.

White religious leaders in the antebellum South often tried to convince black believers that slavery was somehow God's will. But the majority of black churches claimed that God was opposed to slavery and would eventually release them from bondage. Spirituals filled with dramatic stories of miraculous rescues gave the slaves the hope of being relieved from their own hardships. This song makes that hope clear in the line, "Didn't my Lord deliver Daniel, and why not every man?" The implications of such a question were not lost on southern whites, and spirituals were often outlawed. As a result, they were commonly known as "contrabands" throughout the 19th century.

DIDN'T MY LORD DELIVER DANIEL?

Did-n't my Lord de-liv- er Dan - iel, De-liv- er Dan - iel, de-liv- er

Dan - iel, Did-n't my Lord de-liv- er Dan - iel, And why not a ev- e-ry

man? He de- liv-ered Dan - iel from the li-on's den, __

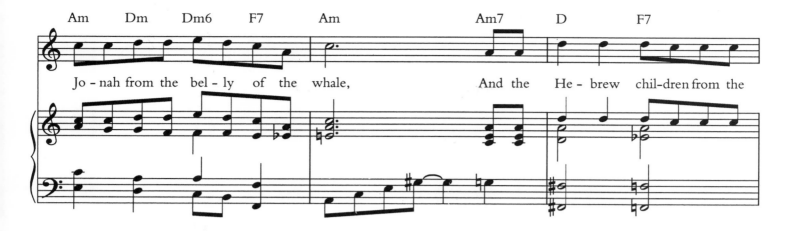

Jo - nah from the bel - ly of the whale, And the He - brew chil-dren from the

fie - ry fur - nace, And why not a ev - e - ry man? Did - n't

D.S. al Fine

The moon run down in a purple stream,
The sun forbear to shine;
And every star will disappear,
King Jesus shall be mine.   *Chorus*

I set my foot on the Gospel ship,
And the ship began for to sail;
It landed me over on Canaan's shore,
And I'll never come back no more.   *Chorus*

This simple and direct spiritual combines the mellifluous *roll* (which blends into the open sound of *Jor*dan) with zipper verses. In one variant of the song, dating from around 1835, the names of certain white ministers who preached passivity and acceptance of white authority were "zipped in" to a mocking version.

ROLL, JORDAN, ROLL

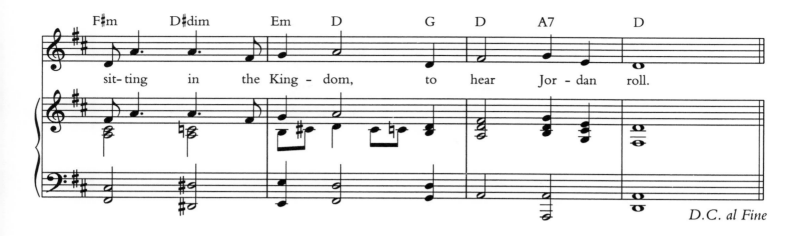

sit-ting in the King - dom, to hear Jor - dan roll.

D.C. al Fine

Jacob, the son of Isaac and the grandson of Abraham, was one of the founders of the Hebrew nation. Once, on his way to visit his father, he was accosted by an angel and wrestled with him all night. Although the angel dislocated Jacob's thigh bone, Jacob held on and refused to let go until he had received a blessing. The angel blessed him and renamed him Israel. His persistence inspired believers who felt that if they could hang on through hard times, they too might be rewarded with a new beginning.

WRESTLE ON, JACOB

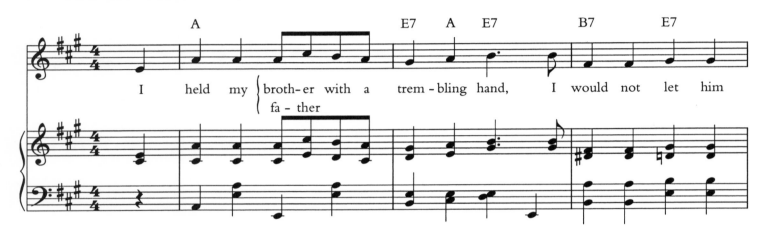

I held my {broth-er with a / fa - ther} trem-bling hand, I would not let him

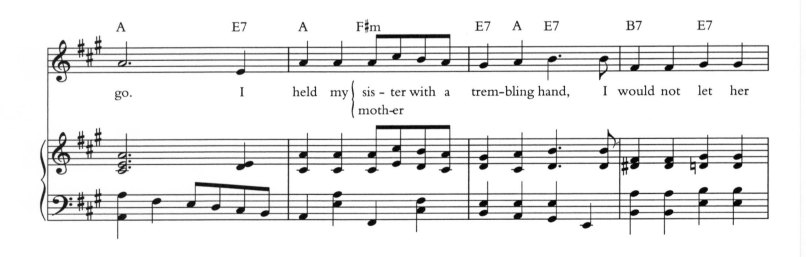

go. I held my {sis - ter with a / moth-er} trem-bling hand, I would not let her

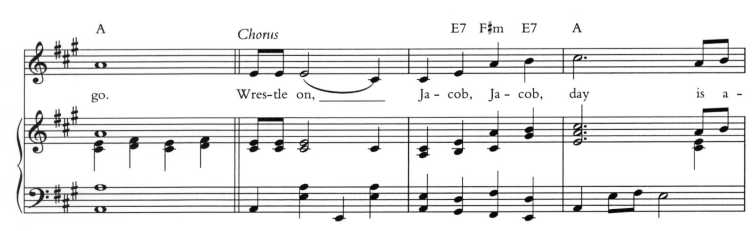

go. Wres-tle on, _____ Ja - cob, Ja - cob, day is a -

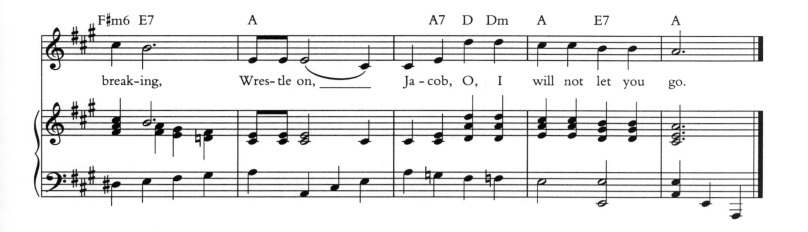

break-ing,   Wres- tle on, _____   Ja - cob,   O,   I   will   not   let   you   go.

For all the hope offered by spirituals, they also evoke powerful feelings of despair. Crying lambs, motherless children, and, in this song, a seemingly never-ending storm, are haunting images of sadness and desolation tempered only by the promise of a better life. "I've Been in the Storm So Long" is an especially heart-wrenching example. The singer knows that prayer will bring some relief, but cannot seem to find time to take that consolation. Even heaven seems a little bleak.

I'VE BEEN IN THE STORM SO LONG

D.S. al Fine

I'll go into Heaven and take my seat,
    O, give me little time to pray,
And-a cast my crown at Jesus' feet,
    O, give me little time to pray.   *Chorus*

A farmhand works with his team on a celery farm in Florida. Before the advent of tractors, farming was often physically exhausting, and farm animals, when available, were an invaluable aid.

O Head all scarred and bleeding,
And heaped with cruel scorn!
O Head so filled with sorrow,
And bound with crown of thorn!
O Head that was so honored,
So lovely fair to see,
And now so low degraded,
My heart goes out to Thee!

So runs the 17th-century German poem that was set to music by Johann Sebastian Bach in his monumental *St. Matthew Passion*. *"He Never Said a Mumblin' Word"* tells the same gruesome story of the torture and crucifixion of Jesus.

HE NEVER SAID A MUMBLIN' WORD

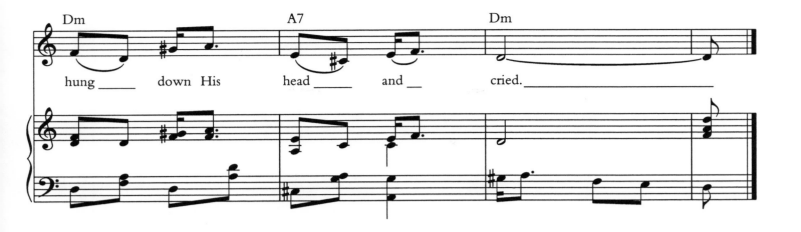

hung _____ down His   head _____ and __   cried. _____

Oh, they crowned Him with a thorny crown . . .

Well, they nailed Him to the cross . . .

Well, they placed Him in the side . . .

Well, the blood came twinklin' down . . .

"Little David, Play on Your Harp" is hard to top for sheer unrestrained joy. The stories told in the verses are exuberantly triumphant tales of righteous men who defeat stronger enemies. David, a young shepherd boy, fells his gigantic opponent with a simple sling. The persistent Joshua destroys the mighty fortress of Jericho. At the end of each verse the chorus exhorts David to play his harp in celebration. This is a true singer's song, proclaiming the defiant power of music in the hands (or the throats) of the weak.

LITTLE DAVID, PLAY ON YOUR HARP

Lit-tle Da-vid, play on your harp, Hal - le - lu, Hal - le - lu, Lit-tle Da-vid,

play on your harp, Hal - le - lu, _____ Lit-tle Da-vid, lu. _____

Fine

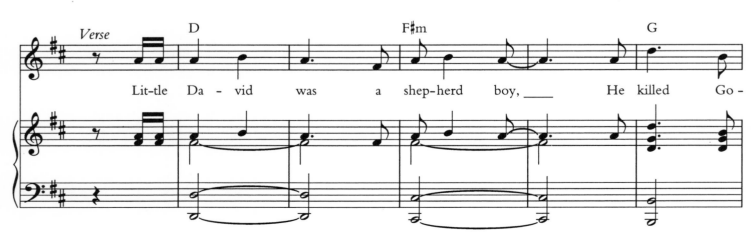

Lit-tle Da - vid was a shep-herd boy, ___ He killed Go -

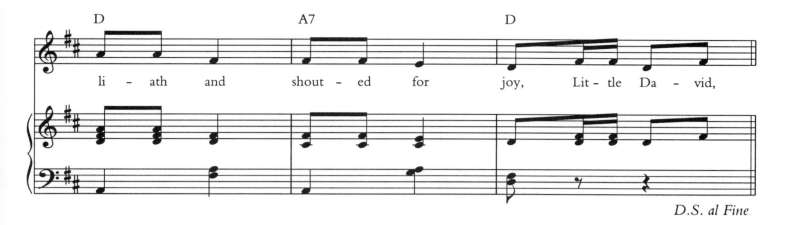

li – ath and shout – ed for joy, Lit – tle Da – vid,

D.S. al Fine

Old Joshua was the son of Nun,
He never would stop till his work was done.   *Chorus*

A boy holds a bag of cotton in this 1823 photograph. The enthusiasm and joy shown by children under even the most trying of circumstances surely inspired the creator of "Little David, Play on Your Harp."

This beautiful, chorale-like spiritual touchingly describes the sacrament of communion. Although the entire church takes part in communion and worship, each individual believer will have to stand before God and be judged on his or her own merits when the time comes. This song, created at a time when white slave owners were trying to destroy the black community and the idea of black personhood, firmly emphasizes the worth of both. It lends itself especially well to four-part harmonization.

LET US BREAK BREAD TOGETHER

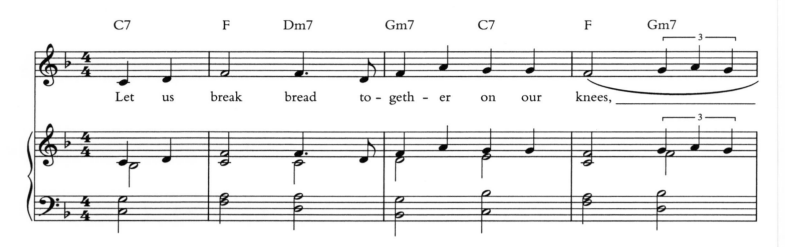

Let us break bread to-geth-er on our knees, ___

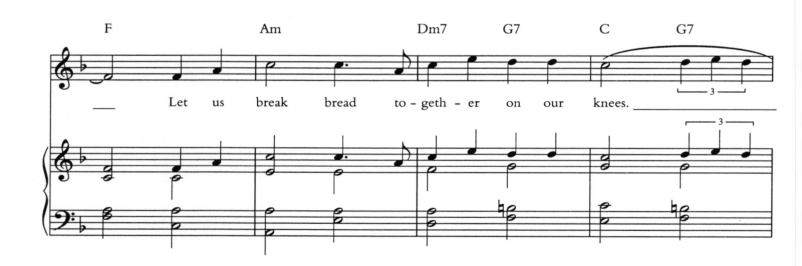

___ Let us break bread to-geth-er on our knees. ___

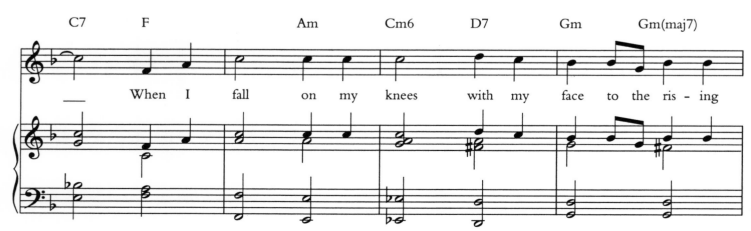

___ When I fall on my knees with my face to the ris-ing

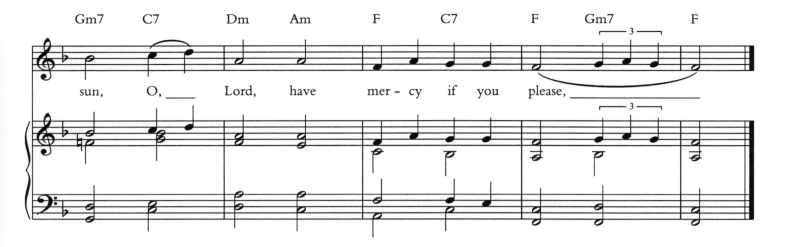

Let us drink wine together . . .

Let us praise God together . . .

Let us all sing together . . .

In biblical times balm of Gilead, made from the resin of an evergreen tree, was prized for its healing powers. In this spiritual the balm is seen as an agent of spiritual solace. Although the present may be disheartening, the promise of a more righteous world encourages the believer to continue in life and in faith. This song is not about ignoring present troubles in vague dreams of a future reward, but about transcending a degrading, dehumanizing day-to-day existence through the strong belief that God will end it one day.

BALM IN GILEAD

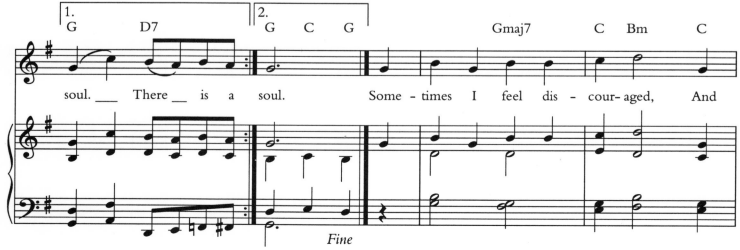

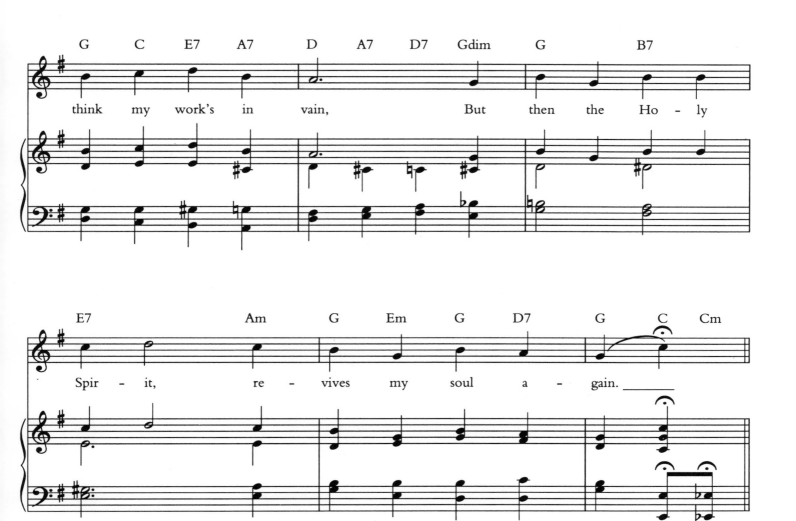

think my work's in vain, But then the Ho - ly

Spir - it, re - vives my soul a - gain. _____

D.C. al Fine

If you can preach like Peter,
If you can pray like Paul,
Go home and tell your neighbor,
"He died to save us all."   *Chorus*

Jerry Silverman is one of America's most prolific authors of music books. He has a B.S. degree in music from the City College of New York and an M.A. in musicology from New York University. He has authored some 100 books dealing with various aspects of guitar, banjo, violin, and fiddle technique, as well as numerous songbooks and arrangements for other instruments. He teaches guitar and music to children and adults and performs in folk-song concerts before audiences of all ages.

Kenneth B. Clark received a Ph.D. in social psychology from Columbia University and is the author of numerous books and articles on race and education. His books include *Prejudice and Your Child*, *Dark Ghetto*, and *Pathos of Power*. Long noted as an authority on segregation in schools, his work was cited by the U.S. Supreme Court in its decision in the historic *Brown v. Board of Education of Topeka* case in 1954. Dr. Clark, Distinguished Professor of Psychology Emeritus at the City University of New York, is the president of Kenneth B. Clark & Associates, a consulting firm specializing in personnel matters, race relations, and affirmative action programs.